"How China defines itself and its greatness as a nation in the future, and how our relationship with China evolves will have an impact on the lives of our own people and, indeed, on global peace and security, as that of any other relationship we have."

President William Jefferson Clinton[1]

In late April 2001, President Bush was asked during an interview if he felt the United States had an obligation to defend Taiwan from an attack by China he responded: "Yes, we do, and the Chinese must understand that." He added that the United States would do "whatever it took to help Taiwan defend herself." When asked about the United States sale of defensive weapons to Taiwan, President Bush pointed out that the shift in defensive focus will help Taiwan defend itself and hold its own until the United States has the time to respond in an attack.[2]

Since 1949, Taiwan and China have maintained separate governments. For the past two decades, the United States has supported the existence of the Republic of China (ROC) government in Taiwan politically, economically and militarily, while diplomatically recognizing the Communist People's Republic of China (PRC) government in Beijing. The geographic separation of Taiwan from the mainland, coupled with the political and military support of the United States, has allowed the ROC government to resist the reunification of China under centralized PRC rule.[3] Although China and Taiwan have both made reunification proposals, a common agreement has not been reached and the issue continues to be the major source of tension between the two governments.

Until recent years, China's military, the People's Liberation Army (PLA), focused primarily on land-based protection of the mainland, but is currently undergoing a major modernization effort to expand its naval and air capabilities. The expansion of the People's Liberation Army Navy (PLAN) may soon make it possible for China to gain and maintain control of the littoral areas around Taiwan and the Taiwan Strait.[4] Recent advances in PRC missile technology have made it possible for China to launch a crippling first-strike attack on

Taiwan with little or no notice. As a result, PRC military advances are rapidly depleting the ability of United States Pacific Command (USPACOM) to defend Taiwan against a Chinese invasion.[5] Accordingly, USPACOM's management of the 'Operational Factors' of space, time and forces in countering PRC military coercion and possible invasion is more critical than ever before to the defense of Taiwan.

This paper will briefly discuss the historical basis for the political and economic differences between Taiwan and the Chinese mainland and examine the events that triggered the two most recent periods of crisis in cross-Strait tensions. It will then analyze China's military modernization efforts and the effects on USPACOM's use of the 'Operational Factors' in planning courses of action to counter Chinese military coercion and/or invasion of Taiwan.[6]

Why China and Taiwan are Different

The struggle for control of Taiwan is not a recent historical development, although the geographic limiting factors that have largely contributed to separation of Taiwan from the Chinese mainland remain as important today as any time in modern history. Large-scale continental Chinese migration to the island of Taiwan began during the 1630's, but the island's geographic separation from the mainland, across nearly one hundred miles of sea strait, kept it essentially isolated from imperial China.[7] A provincial mainland government was not established on the island until 1885, after more than two centuries of essentially little or no continental interference. As a result, the experiences of Taiwan's residents with regard to the government of continental China were substantially different from those of their mainland counterparts. The islanders of Taiwan generally enjoyed more freedom from imperial oppression than their mainland China neighbors.[8]

In 1895, after only ten years of mainland rule, China ceded Taiwan to Japan in a treaty following the first Sino-Japanese war. During its 50 years of Japanese colonial rule, Japan expended considerable effort in public education and developing Taiwan's economy.[9] During the same period, mainland China underwent turbulent periods of revolution, warlord control, Japanese invasion, civil war and peasant rebellion. At the close of WWII, after the Japanese surrender in 1945, Taiwan was highly literate and had a commercially oriented agricultural economy with well-developed transportation and communication.[10] Between 1945 and 1949, Taiwan again fell under the Nationalist Chinese rule and experienced increased corruption and repression that led to local discontent. In 1949, the Communist forces under Mao Zedung defeated the Nationalist forces under Chaing Kai-shek. To escape their Communist agressors, two million refugees, predominately from the Nationalist government, military and business community, fled to Taiwan to reestablished the ROC government.[11]

After 1949, both the PRC and ROC claimed to be the legitimate government of China and each maintained that there was only 'one China'. The struggle for power between China and Taiwan ultimately led to the global superpowers taking sides in the struggle, with the United States supporting the ROC under Chiang and the Soviet Union supporting the PRC under Mao[12] Although the PRC has never actually had any direct governmental control over Taiwan, the Communist leadership has maintained that Taiwan is a renegade province and has repeatedly threatened to invade if Taiwan attempts to declare independence.[13]

The United Nations officially recognized the PRC in October 1971, followed closely by the signing of the first of three Sino-U.S. Joint Communiqués in 1972 acknowledging the 'one China' position.[14] The United States definition of 'one China' has remained intentionally vague for nearly 30 years, but has essentially meant that there is only one nation, with independence for

Taiwan deferred, but to be achieved via peaceful means.[15] For the PRC government, 'one China' means that Taiwan is a subordinate province of the PRC that will maintain a special status upon reunification, while Taiwan maintains that 'one China' should be unified under the common principles of freedom, democracy and common prosperity.[16]

Since 1978, when President Carter shifted official United States recognition from Taiwan to the PRC government, the U.S. has maintained unofficial ties with Taiwan.[17] In reaction to the shift in official United States recognition from Taiwan to Beijing, Congress passed the Taiwan Relations Act in 1979 in an effort to lend continued support to the government of Taiwan. Although the document stops short of any overt promise to defend the island, it states that the United States will supply "such defense articles and defense services in such quantity as may be necessary to enable Taiwan to maintain a sufficient self defense capability." It also states "It is the policy of the United States to maintain the capacity of the United States to resist any resort to force or other forms of coercion that would jeopardize the security, social or economic system of the people on Taiwan."[18]

The Taiwan Strait Crises of 1995-1996 and 1999-2000

The fundamental disagreements between the governments of China and Taiwan since the Communist victory in 1949 have resulted in cross-strait crises in 1954, 1958, 1996 and 2000.[19] In each case the crisis ended without escalating to open warfare, but failed to resolve the underlying differences of opinion that continue to cause political and military friction between the two governments. In the two most recent cases, 1996 and 2000, the origin of the crises centered on China's use of military coercion in reaction to Taiwanese attempts to increase governmental legitimacy and independence. Taiwan's continued movement toward independence runs counter to the long held PRC goals of developing relationships that would ultimately facilitate reunification of Taiwan and the mainland.[20]

In May of 1995, Taiwan's President Li Denghui was allowed an 'unofficial visit' to Cornell University, where he was the graduation speaker. Li's request for a visa was first denied by the Clinton administration in keeping with United States policy, but was later overturned when pressure from Congress forced a State Department reversal. While in the United States, Li repeatedly referred to the "Republic of China on Taiwan" during interviews with the press, which PRC leaders interpreted as an overt reference to independence. Li's visit also coincided with the launching of Taiwan's fifth new Perry-class guided missile frigate and a good will tour of Taiwan Navy ships to other Asian ports.[21] Two months later, China conducted missile tests in the seas 90 miles northeast of Taipei and an underground nuclear test on the Chinese mainland. In November, just prior to the legislative elections in Taiwan, the PRC conducted amphibious exercises and a simulated blockade of Dongshan Island, opposite Taiwan. Shortly thereafter Beijing announced military exercises scheduled for March 1996, coinciding with Taiwan's presidential elections.[22]

In response to the PRC coercion, the United States sent the U.S.S Nimitz (CVN-68) battle group through the Taiwan Strait, the first U.S. carrier to transit the Strait in over 15 years. The Nimitz battle group transit was completed without incident or protest from the PRC. As previously announced, the PRC continued the escalation of military force demonstrations in March including more missile firings, amphibious assaults, air exercises with unprecedented numbers of fighter-attack aircraft and the first deployment of advanced Chinese submarines to the Taiwan Strait.[23] The U.S.S. Independence (CVN-62) and U.S.S. Nimitz battle groups were sent to operate in the area, but remained outside the Taiwan Strait and appeared to have no effect on the conduct or completion of the exercises. The Strait crisis seemed to demonstrate China's repeated assertion that it will not rule out the use of force to resolve the reunification problem that the Communist leadership believes is essential to the future of the PRC.[24]

During the last months of 1996 informal contact between the PRC and Taiwan gradually resumed, but the PRC continued to isolate Taiwan diplomatically. The PRC successfully used its position on the United Nations (UN) Security Council to vote against a peacekeeping mission in Guatemala in order to force a reversal of Guatemala's support for Taiwan's membership in the UN. By the end of 1996, the PRC had also pressured South Africa to break off relations with Taiwan.[25] From 1997 to 1999, relations between the PRC and Taiwan resumed the pre-crisis status quo, with normal levels of trade and relatively peaceful disagreement.

The most recent period of heightened tensions between Taiwan and China began in July of 1999 when President Li again infuriated the PRC leadership with comments of pro ROC legitimacy and independence he made during a radio interview. The interviewer began by stating that Taiwan was considered by the Beijing government to be a "renegade province" and asked how President Li coped with the danger of permanent tensions and threats against his island from the mainland.

> "...The historical fact is that since the establishment of the Chinese communist regime in 1949, it has never ruled the territories under the Republic of China (ROC) jurisdiction: Taiwan, Penghu, Kinmen, and Matsu... The legitimacy of the rule of the country comes from the mandate of the Taiwan people and has nothing to do with the people on the mainland. The 1991 constitutional amendments have placed cross-strait relations as a state-to-state relationship or at least a special state-to-state relationship rather than an internal relationship between a legitimate government and a renegade group, or between a central government and a local government. Thus, the Beijing authorities' characterization of Taiwan as a "renegade province" is historically and legally untrue...Moreover, we will continue to further develop our democratic system, pursue stable economic growth, and actively strengthen contacts with the international community, so as to ensure our survival and development..."[26]

In the wake of the interview, the PRC resumed its policy of coercion against Taiwan and cautioned the United States against interfering in the matter. In February 2000, the PRC again attempted to influence Taiwan's presidential election by warning against declaring independence or resisting reunification. China released an official White Paper entitled The One-China Principle and the Taiwan Issue, which warned, "If the Taiwan authorities refuse…the peaceful settlement of cross-Strait reunification through negotiations, then the Chinese government will only be forced to adopt all drastic measures possible, including the use of force." Regarding the United States support of Taiwan the paper stated, "Regrettably, the United States has repeatedly violated its solemn commitments to China…and continued its sale of advanced arms and military equipment to Taiwan."[27]

As in 1996, PRC coercion appears to have had little effect on the outcome of Taiwan's presidential election. In March 2000, Chen Shui-bian, the leader of the Democratic Progressive Party and formerly a staunch supporter of independence, was elected president. In an effort to spread good will and encourage dialogue with China, President Chin acknowledged in his 2001 New Year's message that the 'one China' principle was endorsed by the Taiwanese constitution, and declared that he would relax controls on Taiwanese investment on the mainland. The following day, he reopened the transport links between the outlying islands of Kinmen and Matsu - the first officially sanctioned direct passage across the Taiwan Strait for more than 50 years.[28]

Though China and Taiwan continue to develop and send proposals for reunification to the other, the fundamental difference between the PRC and Taiwan proposals remains the definition of 'one China'. The PRC proposals stipulate that Taiwan is a province of China and its government will be subordinate to the Communist government in Beijing, while Taiwan continues to push for a state to state relationship that would preserve its democratic government and economy without centralized mainland control.

Modernization of the PRC Military

China has begun an aggressive improvement program for its conventional and nuclear military forces. To facilitate the improvements, China has increased its annual defense budget in excess of 10 percent per year in each of the last eight years and in 2000, the increased totaled 12.7 percent.[29] The long-term goal of the PRC military modernization is to regain military superiority in the Asia-Pacific theater and thereby neutralize the ability of other countries to interfere in the internal affairs of China.[30]

China's purchases of new weapons from Russia, combined with their own research and development programs, have greatly increased the sophistication and power projection capabilities of PLA. To that end, China has fielded an estimated 400-600 new Dong Feng 11 (CSS-7/M-11), Dong Feng 15 (CSS-6/M-9) and CSS-8/M-7 short to medium-range ballistic missiles, with the majority deployed against Taiwan.[31] Long-range Chinese ballistic missiles such as the Dong Feng 21X and Dong Feng 25 have 1,200 and 1,500 mile ranges respectively and are reportedly capable of GPS precision terminal guidance, which could be used to interdict enemy bases, ports and airfields. In the past, the Chinese research and development acquisition cycle was extremely slow, sometimes taking more than a decade to field a new system, resulting in largely obsolete technology. In recent years, the cycle has shortened dramatically with new ballistic and cruise missiles entering service that are near state-of-the-art. According to commercial intelligence sources, it is likely that China currently has operational long-range cruise missiles with stealth characteristics capable of the precision delivery of nuclear and conventional payloads.[32]

The People's Liberation Army Air Force (PLAAF) is gradually replacing its aging aircraft fleet with modern Russian fighter and attack aircraft including the Su-27, Su-30, and Su-37. The acquisition of these advanced aircraft has also provided China with a wide variety of the most advanced Russian air-to-air missiles including the AA-10, AA-11 and AA-12. Additionally, China has acquired Russian-built airborne early warning aircraft and air refueling technology to facilitate over-the-horizon targeting and long-range strike.[33]

The People's Liberation Army Navy (PLAN) forces have received the first of two Sovremenny-class destroyers armed with SS-N-22 anti-ship missiles designed to conduct long range surface-to-surface combat against aircraft carrier battle groups. They have also received several Russian Kilo-class diesel submarines, a very quiet and considerably more capable weapons platform than Chinese built submarines. These submarines can be used to covertly deploy mines, as well as, to conduct anti-submarine and anti-surface operations using torpedoes.[34]

The Operational Factors: Space, Time and Forces

"At any level of war, freedom of action is achieved primarily by properly balancing the factors of space, time and forces…The higher the level of war, the more critical these factors. The term operational factors refer to factors of space, time and force in a given theater of operations."
Dr. Milan N. Vego[35]

The primary task of the Commander in Chief (CINC) USPACOM is to shape the Pacific Theater environment in order to meet the United State's strategic objectives. As such, the United States National Security Strategy for the East Asia-Pacific region specifies the role of the U.S. forces presence in Asia:

"U.S. military presence serves as an important deterrent to aggression…to shape the security environment to keep challenges from developing at all. U.S. force presence mitigates the impact of historical regional tensions and allows the United States to anticipate problems, manage potential threats and encourage peaceful resolution of disputes…Overseas military presence also provides political leaders and commanders the ability to respond rapidly to crises with a flexible array of options."[36]

China's focused military modernization is directly impacting USPACOM's management of time, space and forces in shaping the Pacific Theater. The PLA modernization has shifted away from an emphasis on land-based capabilities in an effort to extend its offensive and defensive capabilities to the littoral and beyond. By expanding the acquisition of modern missile, aircraft and naval programs, Beijing is focusing on programs that will provide the most effective means of 'credible intimidation' by exploiting the military and political weaknesses of Taiwan, the United States and other regional powers.[37] To achieve its goal, the PRC is effectively employing a strategy of incremental gains designed to deny its potential adversaries the ability to maneuver and concentrate forces against China.

Due to the vast distances in the USPACOM area of responsibility (AOR), U.S. forward presence in Japan, Guam, South Korea and Diego Garcia is critical to managing the 'operational factors' in defense of Taiwan. The U.S. relies heavily on overseas basing in Guam, Japan, South Korea and Diego Garcia for housing and logistical support of forward-deployed forces, as well as, alliance relationships with Singapore and Thailand for critical logistical support and transit services for U.S. military aircraft and ships. In recent years, the closures of U.S. Air Force and Navy bases in the Republic of the Philippines have greatly lengthened the U.S. SLOCs, and delayed U.S. forces reaction times in the western Pacific region, lessons that have not been lost on the Chinese.[38] China's close monitoring of the Gulf War allowed them to observe the critical importance of logistical support and rapid deployment force capabilities in the conduct and management of remote-theater conflicts.[39] By limiting the scale of military coercion and the speed of employment, China seeks to capitalize on the factor of time to prevent the concentration of U.S. forces in defense of Taiwan. China's employment of long-range theater ballistic missiles with precision terminal guidance systems is designed to threaten U.S. and allied theater basing, assets and personnel in an effort to make the consequences of coming to Taiwan's aid too costly for the U.S. and its allies.[40]

China's strategic objective is the reunification of Taiwan and the mainland. Reunification would allow Beijing to combine the economic strength of Taiwan's economy with that of the mainland to facilitate China's return to a position of regional political, military and economic supremacy.[41] As such, it is unlikely that China would carry out military attacks that would risk massive destruction of the economic and industrial infrastructure of Taiwan. China's most likely military courses of action consist of the employment of asymmetric force to coerce Taiwan into acquiescence, while the least likely is a physical invasion and occupation of the island. For the purposes of this paper, the scope of the examination of the 'Operational Factors' will be limited to three possible Chinese courses of action against Taiwan: 1. Blockade of Taiwan and the Taiwan Strait. 2. A first-strike missile attack in concert with fixed wing air strikes. 3. A full-scale physical invasion and occupation of the island of Taiwan.

Blockade of Taiwan and the Taiwan Strait

Chinese blockade operations against Taiwan would be designed to choke the island economically and isolate it from U.S. and other allied forces. Taiwan's military planners believe blockade is the most likely form of military coercion that China would employ because it would exert maximum economic pressure without damaging the island's infrastructure.[42] Taiwan's economy and physical infrastructure are based on import and export trade and could not survive without the importation of raw industrial materials and the export of finished manufactured products. Perhaps most importantly, Taiwan's limited

natural resources are insufficient to sustain its densely populated urban cities, making the

island dependent on imported petroleum products and natural gas for approximately 90

percent of its energy needs, as well as, food and other basic resources.[43] Taiwan's two

major ports, Kaohsiung and Keelung, are the second and third busiest ports in Asia

respectively and over 75 percent of the island's fuel requirements are imported through

Keelung.[44]

In keeping with China's desire to avoid third party intervention, blockade operations

would most likely begin gradually by declaring maritime closure or exclusion areas and use

of PLAN surface combatants to interdict shipping in the Taiwan Strait and SLOCs into

Taiwan. As the flow of commercial shipping to and from Taiwan began to slow, PLAN

submarines could covertly mine the entrances to Taiwan's commercial ports. To completely

stop the flow of shipping traffic, submarines could interdict shipping in the SLOCs with

anti-surface torpedoes.

Taiwan's Air Force and Navy assets are qualitatively superior, but quantitatively

inferior to China's because of the large disparity in fighter aircraft and submarines.[45]

Accordingly, Taiwan's military deterrent and counter blockade options would rely on

localized air superiority and antisubmarine warfare. Air power would be used to protect

Taiwan's Navy surface combatants from Chinese air attacks with launched anti-surface

missiles, as well as, to provide protective combat air patrol (CAP) for Taiwan's anti-

submarine aircraft and helicopters. Although Taiwan has eight Knox-class anti-submarine

frigates and nine S-70 Seahawk anti-submarine helicopters, the quantitative disparity in submarines is such that China could carry out an effective blockade with less than one third of its total submarine force.[46]

During past Taiwan Strait crises, the platform of choice for the U.S. has been the Navy aircraft carrier battle group (CVBG). In a high-threat area filled with hostile submarines and aircraft, the CVBG would need anti-submarine protection from forward-deployed U.S. submarines and long-range P-3 anti-submarine aircraft, as well as, unconstrained open seas for maneuver and carrier aircraft operations. Of note, the elimination of anti-submarine warfare (ASW) systems from S-3B aircraft has left U.S. CVBGs without an organic fixed-wing anti-submarine capability. As such, U.S. force protection would likely dictate that the CVBG operate east of Taiwan in the Philippine Sea, well outside the effective reach of Chinese fighter-attack aircraft and the concentrated submarine threat.[47]

If U.S. CVBG assets are sent to the aid of Taiwan, time will have a significant role in the U.S. forces reaction to the blockade. Currently, USS Kitty Hawk stationed in Japan, is the only U.S. Pacific Fleet carrier stationed outside the continental U.S. (CONUS). If there are no constraints on immediate deployment, the USS Kitty Hawk could reach Taiwan in three and one half days. If a carrier battle group transits from the west-coast of the U.S., it will take approximately 14 ½ days to reach Taiwan from Bremerton, Washington or 16 ½ days from San Diego, California. Diverting a carrier from the Persian Gulf to Taiwan, as in the 1996 Taiwan Strait crisis, takes approximately 12 days.[48] U.S. Navy P-3 aircraft are forward-deployed to Japan and Diego Garcia and could be repositioned to Kadena Air Base in southern Japan within 24-48 hours.

A First-Strike Missile and Air Attack

For the past decade, China has continuously increased the size and effectiveness of its missile forces with particular emphasis on short and medium range ballistic missiles. As discussed in a previous section, China has fielded an estimated 400-600 new short to medium-range ballistic missiles, with the majority deployed against Taiwan. Using time and forces to the maximum advantage of the attacker, these missiles could be launched in high volume against Taiwan's command and control nodes (C^2), airfields (aircraft ramps and runways), fuel storage facilities, air defense facilities, naval facilities and combatant ships in port. Even if Taiwan successfully employs its active missile defenses, China's overwhelming volume of offensive missiles would likely inflict crippling damage on the island's military defenses.

In April 1999, commercial intelligence sources discovered that China had built a simulation air base identical to the ROC's largest air base, Ching Chuang Kang, in central Taiwan. The replica base, which was built next to the Dingxin air base in China's northwestern province of Gangsu, was believed to be designed for training Chinese pilots and missile units for a possible attack on Taiwan.[49] Gaining and maintaining air superiority will be an essential element of a successful first-strike attack, but will present a major challenge for the PLAAF.

China's air force has a substantial numerical advantage in aircraft, but is qualitatively inferior to the modern equipment of Taiwan's air force. A large portion of the PLAAF consists of older technology F-5, F-6, F-7 and F-8 fighter aircraft that were designed and built in the 1960's and 1970's.[50] China's ability to concentrate large numbers of fighter and attack aircraft against Taiwan is constrained by the relatively small 370-mile combat radius of the older aircraft and by the limited capacity of airfields in China's Fujian and Guangdong provinces. China is reportedly building airfields in the Nanjing Military Region adjacent to Taiwan, but airfield capacity within reach of the island will still be limited.[51] According to National Imagery and Mapping Agency charts ONC H-12 and ONC J-12, there are eight airports on the mainland within 150 nautical miles of the western coast of Taiwan. Movement of aircraft and support equipment into those airfields prior to the attack would be vulnerable to military and commercial satellite imaging and could severely reduce the surprise effect of the strike by allowing Taiwan and the United States time to mobilize.[52]

As depicted in Table 2, Taiwan is equipped with modern state-of-the art fighter aircraft built by the United States and France. "Assuming a loss ratio of 10:1, as during the Korean War, or 16:1, as during the 1958 Taiwan Strait crisis, then China would lose most of its aircraft either to Taiwan's fighters or to its layered surface-to-air missile defenses."[53] Although intelligence analysts are mixed in their estimates of Chinese losses, the final outcome would most likely be determined by the effectiveness of the missile strike in disabling Taiwan's airfields.

United States military reaction to a Chinese first strike missile and air attack on Taiwan will likely be limited to post-strike battle damage assessment (BDA). Unless satellite and other intelligence sources detected a buildup or movement of aircraft prior to the strike, it is unlikely that U.S. forces could react in time to deter the attack or interdict on behalf of Taiwan. The closest U.S. fighter aircraft in theater are U.S. Air Force F-15s stationed on Kadena Air Base in southern Japan, approximately 1000 miles northwest of Taiwan. The reaction times for U.S. CVBGs mentioned in the blockade scenario would also apply in a missile scenario. Although CVBG transit times could begin prior to the attack if sufficient intelligence cueing was received, it is unlikely that a CVBG could reach Taiwan prior to an attack.

Amphibious Invasion and Vertical Envelopment

The geographic characteristics of Taiwan provide both advantages and disadvantages for defense with regard to the dynamics of space. Located approximately 100 miles east of the eastern coast of China, Taiwan enjoys an insular geostrategic position in relation to the mainland.[53] Taiwan's physical separation from the Chinese mainland is the single most advantageous factor of space in defending the island because the invasion force must first cross the Taiwan Strait by sea or air.

An invasion of Taiwan would be an extremely high-risk option for the PLA and would most likely cause catastrophic damage to the public and industrial infrastructure of the island. Any attempt to land forces on the heavily defended island would be preceded by preparatory attacks to isolate the island, soften the military resistance and gain air superiority over Taiwan and the Strait. The preparatory offensive would probably consist of a combination of the blockade and missile/air attack scenarios previously discussed.

The population density of Taiwan is second only to Bangladesh, with approximately 60 percent of the total population concentrated in four city areas: Taipaei, Kao-hsiung, Tai-chung, and Tai-nan. Occupation of Taiwan's densely populated urban areas would be a formidable task for PLA ground forces given that the vast majority of the population would be considered hostile. Although the physical characteristics of the island would add to the difficulty of the defense, they would also restrict the mobility of the invading land force.[54] Approximately 67 percent of Taiwan is covered in foothills and mountainous terrain. The

Central Mountain Range separates the island from east to west, which combined with the islands elongated shape, provides very limited depth for defense. Few roads traverse the mountain range severely limiting movement and maneuver in the mountainous regions. Off-road travel in the mountains can only be accomplished on foot or by air, as the steep, rough terrain prevents any use of land vehicles.[55]

China maintains a substantial quantitative advantage in PRC active forces with over two million army troops on active duty compared with 200,000 in Taiwan.[56] The main limiting factor for the Chinese invasion force would be the amphibious lift capability to land the invasion force on the island. Although intelligence reports of PLAN amphibious capability vary widely, China's 343 amphibious ships have a total troop capacity of 55,970 and a tank capacity of 246.[57] Considering that the ROC maintains 200,000 army troops on active duty and 1.5 million in reserve, it seems highly unlikely that a PLA invasion force with a 4:1 disadvantage in troops could overwhelm the highly fortified and well defended island.[58]

Additionally, China's mobilization and logistical movements in preparation for an amphibious invasion would be extremely hard to conceal from military and commercial imaging satellites and other intelligence sources. Taking advantage of intelligence cueing prior to the start of an invasion could allow Taiwan and the United States precious mobilization and preparation time, possibly allowing U.S. CVBGs to reach Taiwan prior to or during an attack. PLAN amphibious ships would be extremely vulnerable to carrier and land based aircraft attack and PLAAF forces would have difficulty establishing air supremacy against Taiwan Air Force fighters and U.S. CVBG aircraft working in concert to defend the island.

Conclusion

Although Chinese missile technology is advancing rapidly toward state-of-the-art, PLAN and PLAAF capabilities are largely based on antiquated weapons systems that are technologically inferior to U.S. and ROC systems, as well as, those systems used by our primary Pacific Theater allies Japan and South Korea. As China continues to advance its weapons systems technology and exploit its asymmetric capabilities, it will become increasingly harder for USPACOM to maintain the delicate balance of power in the Asia-Pacific region.

In April 2001, President Bush announced approval for the sale of U.S. weapons to Taiwan including: anti-submarine aircraft, counter-mine helicopters, destroyers, missiles and diesel submarines in an effort to counter the expanding military threat from China.[59] U.S. approval of the purchase came in the wake of an in-depth USPACOM examination of current ROC and PRC capabilities and recommendations made by the CINC. U.S. approval for the sale reflected the military, political and economic importance of maintaining open sea lines of communication (SLOC) for Taiwan and the Asia-Pacific region, as well as, maintenance of the delicate balance of force between China and Taiwan.[60]

For the immediate future, the keys to maintaining the USPACOM's ability to defend Taiwan against a Chinese invasion are: 1. Maintenance of U.S. overseas presence and the continued expansion of regional alliances that will allow U.S. forces to remain agile and to overcome China's strategy of area denial. 2. Continued U.S. participation in bi-lateral and multi-national military exercises such as Cobra Gold, Rim of the Pacific (RIMPAC) and Ulchi Focus Lens (UFL), as well as, military to military training exchanges with non-participant countries to continue to strengthen U.S. relations in the region. 3. As newly emerging technology becomes available, USPACOM should exploit advances in C^4I, network-centric warfare and theater ballistic missile defense (TBMD) to shape the theater and reduce China's localized advantages in the 'operational factors' of time and space.

NOTES

[1] United States Pacific Command, <u>Asia-Pacific Economic Update</u>, (Pearl Harbor, HI: United States Pacific Command, Summer 1996), "Forward".

[2] Neil King, Jr., "Bush Sows Confusion As He Pledges to Defend Taiwan, Then Backs Off", <u>Wall Street Journal</u>, 26 April 2001, <http://www.ebird.dtic.mil/Apr2001/e20010426policy.htm.> [26 April 2001].

[3] Douglas Porch, "The Taiwan Strait Crisis of 1996 Strategic Implications for the United States Navy," <u>Naval War College Review</u>, Summer 1999, Vol. LII, No. 3, 23.

[4] Strategic Forecasting, "United States-China: Competing for Regional Influence", 18 April 2000, <http://www.stratfor.com/services/giu2001/041801.asp.>, [26 April 2001].

[5] Taiwan Studies Institute, "Military Balance Shifting in Taiwan Strait", 29 March 2000, <http://www.taiwanstudies.org/news_commentary/view_story.php3?130.> [26 April 2001].

[6] Milan Vego, <u>Operational Warfare</u>, (United States Naval War College, Newport, RI, 2000) 29.

[7] John W. Garver, <u>Face Off</u>, (Seattle, WA: University of Washington Press 1997), 19.

[8] Muthiah Alagappa, ed., <u>Asian Security Practice: Material and Ideation Influences</u> (Stanford, CA: Stanford University Press, 1998), 288-290. From an article by Roger Cliff, entitled "Taiwan: In the Dragon's Shadow."

[9] U.S. Department of State, "Background Notes-Taiwan", Bureau of East Asian and Pacific Affairs, October 2000, 1.
<http://www.state.gov/www/background_notes/taiwan_1098_bgn.html.> [26 April 2001].
Also Garver, 19.

[10] U.S. Department of State, 2.
Also Garver, 19.

[11] Central Intelligence Agency, "CIA World Fact Book 2000", Taiwan,
<http://www.cia.gov/cia/publications/factbook/geos/tw.html>, [08 April 2000].
Also U.S. Department of State, 2.

[12] Garver, 19.

[13] Deutsche Welle radio: English: News &Current Affairs, Interview with Lee Teng-hui, President of the Republic of China (Taiwan), <http://www.dwelle.de/english/interview.html.> [08 April 2000].

[14] The first communiqué was the "Shanghai Communiqué", signed by President Nixon on February 27, 1972. It recognized 'one China' and that Taiwan was part of China. It also announced the withdrawal of U.S. forces and bases from Taiwan. The second communiqué was the "Joint Communiqué on the Establishment of Diplomatic Relations" signed by President Carter on January 1, 1979. The third communiqué was "The United States-People's Republic of China Communiqué" signed by President Reagan on August 7, 1982. It stated that the United States did not seek to carry out long term arms sales to Taiwan and that future sales would not exceed the levels of previous years.

[15] David E. Sanger, "Bush Tells Beijing the U.S. Ready to Defend Taiwan", New York Times, April 26, 2001, p. 1 <http://www.ebird.dtic.mil/April2001/e20010426bush.htm>, [26 April 2001].

[16] Alexander Chieh-Cheng, Chinese Maritime Modernization and its Security Implications. (Ann Arbor, MI: University Microfilms International, 1996), 353-354.

[17] Ben Barber, "Bush's Remarks Leave Doubt in U.S. Policy", The Washington Times, 26 April 2001, <http://www.ebird.dtic.mil/April 2001/e20010426policy.htm.> [26 April 2001].

[18] Steven Mufson, "President Pledges Defense of Taiwan", The Washington Post, 26 April 2001, <http://www.ebird.dtic.mil/April 2001/e20010426president.htm.>, [26 April 2001].

[19] Porch, 15.

[20] Ibid, 16.

[21] Ibid, 18.

[22] Ibid, 19.

[23] Ibid, 21.

[24] Ibid, 25.

[25] James R. Lilley and Chuck Downs, Crisis in the Taiwan Strait, (Washington, D.C.: National Defense University, 1999), 37-38.

[26] Deutsche Welle radio: English: News & Current Affairs, Interview with Lee Teng-hui, President of the Republic of China (Taiwan), <http://www.dwelle.de/english/interview.html.> [08 April 2000].

[27] Congress, House, House Armed Services Committee, National Security Report, "China in the Ascendancy: A growing threat to U.S. Security?," Staff Report, Volume 4, Issue 2, May 2000, 2.

[28] Jane's Information Group, Limited, <u>Jane's Sentinel Security Assessment: China and Northeast Asia. April 2001</u>, (Surrey, England, 2001).

[29] Congress, House, 3.

[30] Porch, 23.

[31] Jane's Information Group, Limited, <u>Jane's Sentinel Security Assessment: China and Northeast Asia. December 2000</u>, (Surrey, England, 2000).

[32] Jane's Information Group, December 2000.

[33] Jane's Information Group, December 2000.

[34] Congress, House, 3.

[35] Vego, 29.

[36] Department of Defense, <u>United States Security Strategy for East Asia and Pacific Region</u>, (Washington, D.C. 1998), 4., <http://www.defenselink.mil/pubs/easr98/> [10 May 2001].

[37] Department of Defense, <u>U.S. Department of Defense Report to Congress Pursuant to the FY99 Appropriations Bill</u>, (Washington, D.C: 1999), 3., <http://www.defenselink.mil/pubs/twstrait_02261999.html.> [08 April 2001].

[38] Porch, 20.

[39] Charles T. Mangum, "China's Emergence as a World Power: Effect on United States' Sustaining Base," (Unpublished Research Paper, United States Army Management Staff College, March 1998), 7.

[40] Robert Ford, CAPT, USN, Chief of Staff, Commander ASW Forces U.S. Pacific Fleet and Commander Task Force Twelve, telephone conversation with the author, 11 May 2001. CAPT Ford was a member of the USPACOM evaluation team sent to Taiwan in FY 2000 to evaluate ROC military readiness, defense needs and arms requirements. His team produced a report with recommendations for U.S. foreign military sales to Taiwan.

[41] Ford, telephone.

[42] Gary Klintworth, "Chinese Defense Modernization and the Security of Taiwan, (Rand Corporation, Santa Monica, CA, 2000) 158. <http://www.rand.org/publications/CF/CF137/CF137.chap9.pdf>, [26 April 2001].

[43] Central Intelligence Agency, "CIA World Fact Book 2000", Taiwan, <http://www.cia.gov/cia/publications/factbook/geos/tw.html>, [08 April 2000].

[44] Gary Klintworth, 158-159.

[45] Dan Morgan, "New Life for Diesel Sub Builders?," The Washington Post, 26 April 2001, <http:// www.ebird.dtic.mil/apr2001e20010426builders.htm.> [26 April 2001]. Also Jane's Information Group, December 2000.

[46] Department of Defense, U.S. Department of Defense Report to Congress Pursuant to the FY99 Appropriations Bill, (Washington, D.C: 1999), 9., <http://www.defenselink.mil/pubs/twstrait_02261999.html.> [08 April 2001]. Also Gary Klintworth, 159.

[47] Ford, telephone.

[48] Ford, telephone.

[49] Jane's Information Group, December 2000. Also Jane's Information Group, April 2001.

[50] Lacy H. Bartee, Jr., "Possible U.S. Navy Responses to People's Republic of China Military Action Against Taiwan", (Unpublished Research Paper, U.S. Army Command and Staff College, Fort Levenworth, KS: 2000), 36.

[51] Ibid, 36.

[52] Ford, telephone.

[53] Vego, 33-42. Also Central Intelligence Agency, CIA World Fact Book 2000.

[54] Federation of American Scientists, "Taiwan Strait", (Washington D.C., 2001), 1. <www.fas.org/man/dod-101/ops/taiwan-geo.htm.>, [26 April 2001].

[55] Ibid, 2.

[56] Jane's Information Group, 1999.

[57] Jane's Information Group, 1999 Also Asia Pacific Defense Reporter, 61.

[58] Jane's Information Group, 1999, 76-79 and 516, 525.

[59] Mufson, 1.
Also, Sanger, 1.

[60] Ford, telephone.

BIBLIOGRAPHY

Abitante, George. "China's Military Modernization Effects of Operational Art."
Unpublished Research Paper, United States Naval War College, Newport, RI: 1999.

Alagappa, Muthiah, ed. Asian Security Practice: Material and Ideational Influences.
Stanford, CA: Stanford University Press, 1998.

Ahrari, Dr. Ehsan. 1998. China's naval forces look to extend their blue water
reach. Jane's Intelligence Review 10, no. 4 (April): 31-36.

Barber, Ben, "Bush's Remarks Leave Doubt in U.S. Policy", The Washington Times,
26 April 2001, <http://www.ebird.dtic.mil/April 2001/e20010426policy.htm.>
[26 April 2001].

Bartee, Lacy H., "Possible U.S. Navy Responses to People's Republic of China Military Action
Against Taiwan", Unpublished Research Paper, U.S. Army Command and Staff College,
Fort Levenworth, KS: 2000.

Bernstein, Richard, and Munro, Ross H., The Coming Conflict With China.
New York, NY: Vintage Press. 1998.

Blair, Dennis C. "Remarks by Admiral Dennis C. Blair, USN at the Institute of
Strategic and International Studies." Lecture. Kuala Lumpur, Malaysia: 8 September
1999. <http://www.pacom.mil/ref/past/99/sst/sst-05.htm> [26 April 2001].

Bordwell, John H. "China's Military Modernization: To What Extent Can the
People's Liberation Army Fight at the Operational Level of War?" Unpublished
Research Paper, United States Naval War College, Newport, RI: 1999.

Alexander Chieh-Cheng, Chinese Maritime Modernization and its Security Implications.
Ann Arbor, MI: University Microfilms International, 1996.

Clark, Cal. The 2000 Taiwan presidential elections. AsiaSociety.org Digest.
March 2000. <http://www.asiasociety.org/publications/taiwan_
Elections.html#chinarel.>, [26 April 2001].

Central Intelligence Agency, "CIA World Fact Book 2000", Taiwan,
<http://www.cia.gov/cia/publications/factbook/geos/tw.html>, [08 April 2000].

Congress, House, House Armed Services Committee, National Security Report, "China in the
Ascendancy: A growing threat to U.S. Security?," Staff Report, Volume 4, Issue 2,
May 2000.

Dangerous Moves: Russia's sale of missile destroyers to China. The Heritage
    Foundation: 20 February 1997, ASC Backrounder No. 146.
    <http://www.heritage.org/library/categories/forpol/asc146.html. [26 April 2001].

David, Gerral K. "Defending Taiwan: United States Pacific Command's Deterrent and
    Engagement Options" Unpublished Research Paper, United States Naval War College,
    Newport, RI: 2000.

Deutsche Welle radio: English: News and Current Affairs. Interview with Lee
    Teng-hui, President of the Republic of China (Taiwan).
    <http://www.dwelle.de/english/interview.html.> [26 April 2001].

Eckholm, Erik. "China denies it bought Israeli radar", New York Times, 17
    November 1999. <http://ebird.dtic.mil/Nov1999/e199991117china.
    Html. [26 April 2001].

Fisher, Richard D., "China increases its missile forces while opposing U.S.
    missile defense." The Heritage Foundation, 7 April 1999, ASC Backgrounder No. 1268.
    <http://www.heritage.org/library/backgrounder/bg1268.html.> [26 April 2001]

Ford, Robert Chief of Staff, Commander ASW Forces U.S. Pacific Fleet and Commander Task
    Force Twelve, telephone conversation with the author, 11 May 2001.

Garver, John W., Face-off: China, the United States, and Taiwan's
    Democratization. Seattle: University of Washington Press, 1987.

Harris, Jerry D., Jr. "Chinese defense modernization and the defense of
    Taiwan: Implications for the USAF." Unpublished Thesis, United States Air Force Air
    University, Maxwell AFB, AL, 1998.

Hickey, Dennis Van Vranken. United States-Taiwan Security Ties. Westport,
    CT: Praeger Publishers, 1994.

Howard, Russell D., The Chinese People's Liberation Army: "Short arms
    and slow legs." INSS Occasional Paper 28, Regional Security Series. USAF Institute for
    Strategic Studies, USAF Academy, Colorado, September 1999.

Hugar, Wayne R., "How far will the dragon swim?," Naval Institute Proceedings, March 1999,
    48-51.

Jianxiang Bi. "Managing Taiwan Operations in the Twenty-first Century: Issues
    and Options." Naval War College Review, Autumn 1999, Vol. LII, No. 4,
    pp. 30-58.

King, Jr., Neil, "Bush's Sows Confusion As He Pledges to Defend Taiwan, Then Backs Off",
    Wall Street Journal, 26 April 2001,
    <http://www.ebird.dtic.mil/Apr2001/e20010426policy.htm> [26 April 2001].

Lilley, James R., and Downs, Chuck. 1997. Crisis in the Taiwan Strait.
    Washington, D.C.: National Defense University.

Lilley, James R., and Shambaugh, David, ed. China's Military Faces the Future.
    Washington, D. C.: East Gate, 1999.

Mangum, Charles T. "China's Emergence as a World Power: Effect on United States'
    Sustaining Base," Unpublished Research Paper: The Army Management Staff College,
    March 1998.

Mufson, Steven, "President Pledges Defense of Taiwan", The Washington Post, 26 April 2001,
    <http://www.ebird.dtic.mil/April 2001/e20010426president.htm.>, [26 April 2001].

Nolt, James H.,"The China-Taiwan military balance," Taiwan Security
    Research 2000 <http://www.taiwansecurity.org/IS/IS-012000-Nolt.html.
    26 April 2001.

O'Hanlon, Michael, "Can China Conquer Taiwan?" International Security, Fall 2000, Vol. 25,
    No. 2.

Porch, Douglas. "The Taiwan Strait Crisis of 1996: Strategic Implications for the
    United States Navy." Naval War College Review, Summer 1999, Vol. LII, No. 3, pp. 15-
    48.

Powell, Stewart M. and Rosenberg, Eric. "If Taiwan Is Attacked, What Does U.S.
    Do?" San Francisco Examiner, 8 May 2000, p. 12. <http://www.ebird.dtic.mil/cgi-
    bin/ebird. [26 April 2001].

"President Jiang: 'Taiwan independence' Will Not Be Tolerated." 30 March 2000.
    <http://www.china-embassy.org/taiwan/tw004.htm> [26 April 2001].

Ren, Yue. "China's dilemma in cross-strait crisis management," Asian
    Affairs, An American Review 24, no. 3. (Fall 2000) 131-151.

Sanger, David E., "Bush Tells Beijing the U.S. Ready to Defend Taiwan", New York Times,
    April 26, 2001, p. 1 <http://www.ebird.dtic.mil/April2001/e20010426bush.htm>,
    [26 April 2001].

Slavin, Barbara, and Steven Komarow. "China's military upgrade may raise
    stakes in Taiwan." USA Today, 19 November 1999: 16.

Stokes, Mark A., "China's strategic modernization: Implications
    for the United States," Strategic Studies Institute, U.S. Army War College,
    Carlisle, PA, September 1999.

Strategic Forecasting, "United States-China: Competing for Regional Influence", 18 April 2000,
    <http://www.stratfor.com/services/giu2001/041801.asp.>, [26 April 2001].

Taiwan Studies Institute, "Military Balance Shifting in Taiwan Strait", 29 March 2000,
    <http://www.taiwanstudies.org/news_commentary/view_story.php3?130.>
    [26 April 2001].

United States Pacific Command, Asia-Pacific Economic Update, Pearl Harbor, HI:
    United States Pacific Command, (Summer 1996), "Forward".

"United States Pacific Command at a Glance." USPACOM at a Glance Fact Sheet.
    <http://www.pacom.mil/about/pacom/htm.> [26 April 2001].

U.S. Department of State, "Background Notes-Taiwan", Bureau of East Asian and Pacific
    Affairs, October 2000.

Vego, Milan, Operational Warfare, United States Naval War College, Newport, RI: 2000.

Vogel, Ezra F., ed. Living With China: U.S.-China Relations in the Twenty-first
    Century. New York: W. W. Norton & Company, 1997.

Wortzel, Larry M., "China's military potential," Strategic Studies Institute, United States
    Army War College, Carlisle, PA, 2 October 1998.

Yu, Peter Kien-hong. "The Chinese PLA's perception of an invasion of
    Taiwan" New York, NY: Contemporary US-Asia Research Institute, 1996.

Zalamea, Ulysses O. "EAGLES and DRAGONS at Sea: The inevitable Strategic
    Collision Between the United States and China." Unpublished Research Paper, U.S.
    Naval War College, Newport, RI: 1996.

1999. "The Chinese armed forces in the 21st century," Strategic Studies Institute,
    U.S. Army War College, Carlisle, PA, December.